Start with Art

Drawing

Isabel Thomas

www.raintreepublishers.co.uk
Visit our website to find out more information about Raintree books.

To order:
☎ Phone 0845 6044371
🗎 Fax +44 (0) 1865 312263
🖳 Email myorders@raintreepublishers.co.uk

Customers from outside the UK please telephone +44 1865 312262

Raintree is an imprint of Capstone Global Library Limited, a company incorporated in England and Wales having its registered office at 7 Pilgrim Street, London, EC4V 6LB – Registered company number: 6695582

Edited by Dan Nunn, Rebecca Rissman, and Catherine Veitch
Designed by Richard Parker
Picture research by Mica Brancic and Hannah Taylor
Originated by Capstone Global Library
Printed and bound in China by South China Printing Company Ltd

ISBN 978 1 406 22406 1
15 14 13 12 11
10 9 8 7 6 5 4 3 2 1

Acknowledgements
We would like to thank the following for permission to reproduce photographs: Alamy Images p. 4 (Cultura); © Capstone Publishers pp. 7, 8, 14, 20, 21, 22, 23 – tools (Karon Dubke), 15 (Erik Lervold); Corbis pp. 9 (Christie's Images), 11 (© Succession Picasso/DACS, London 2011); Rex Features p. 6 (Nils Jorgensen); Scala pp. 10, 13, 16 (© The Metropolitan Museum of Art/Art Resource New York); Shutterstock pp. 12 (© Studio 37), 17 (Václav Tauš), 23 – creative (© Monkey Business Images [Cultura]), 23 – gallery (© Shamleen), 23 – portrait (© Studio 37), 23 – self-portrait (© re_bekka), 23 – surface (©Evgenia Sh.), 23 – texture (© Konstantin Sutyagin); The Bridgeman Art Library pp. 5, 18 (Graphische Sammlung Albertina, Vienna, Austria), 19 (Private Collection/Photo © Lefevre Fine Art Ltd., London).

Front cover photograph of Self Portrait, 1912 (charcoal on paper) by Juan Gris (1887–1927), Lefevre Gallery reproduced with permission of The Bridgeman Art Library (Private Collection/Photo © Lefevre Fine Art Ltd., London). Back cover photograph of pencils, card etc reproduced with permission of © Capstone Publishers (Karon Dubke). Back cover photograph of portrait of a girl reproduced with permission of Shutterstock (© Studio 37).

Every effort has been made to contact copyright holders of material reproduced in this book. Any omissions will be rectified in subsequent printings if notice is given to the publisher.

All the Internet addresses (URLs) given in this book were valid at the time of going to press. However, due to the dynamic nature of the Internet, some addresses may have changed, or sites may have changed or ceased to exist since publication. While the author and publisher regret any inconvenience this may cause readers, no responsibility for any such changes can be accepted by either the author or the publisher.

Contents

What is a drawing?.................................... 4

Where can I see drawings?...................... 6

What do people use to make drawings?... 8

How do people make drawings? 10

Why do people make drawings? 12

What else do people draw? 14

What can drawings show?...................... 16

What is a self-portrait?............................ 18

Start to draw! 20

Glossary 23

Find out more... 24

Index 24

Some words are shown in bold, **like this**. You can find out what they mean by looking in the glossary.

What is a drawing?

A drawing is a picture made up of lines and other marks.

Artists make drawings to show what they see or think.

This drawing of an elephant is 400 years old.

There were no cameras then. Drawings showed people what different animals looked like.

Where can I see drawings?

You can see drawings in a museum or **gallery**.

Many visitors come to look at drawings by famous artists.

Drawings are all around you, too.

Drawings in books show you what people in stories look like.

What do people use to make drawings?

People draw with all these **tools**.

They draw on flat **surfaces**, such as paper or card.

Many Chinese artists draw with ink.

They use the ink to draw fat lines and thin lines.

How do people make drawings?

Drawings are made of different lines and shapes.

The straight lines, curved lines, and dots give this drawing **texture**.

This picture has long, curvy lines.

The artist added shapes and colours
to finish this picture of a dove.

Why do people make drawings?

Drawings are a good way to show people your ideas.

You can draw things that you see, know, or remember.

Many artists draw things they see,
such as people, places, and objects.

Their drawings tell us about other
times and places.

What else do people draw?

Some artists draw made-up things.

It is fun to be **creative**.

You can use drawings to tell a story.

A cartoon uses pictures instead of words.

What can drawings show?

Some artists make their drawings look real.

This **portrait** shows us what the shoemaker really looked like.

Drawings do not have to look real.

The shapes and lines in this drawing
show a woman's face.

What is a self-portrait?

If you cannot find anything to draw, try drawing yourself!

A famous artist drew this **self-portrait** when he was a boy.

Artists use self-portraits to tell us about themselves.

Do you think this artist was a happy or a grumpy person?

Start to draw!

Some artists learn to draw by feeling things instead of looking at them.

1. Ask a friend to blindfold you.

2. Get them to give you an object without telling you what it is.

3. Feel the object carefully, and then give it back to your friend.

4. Take your blindfold off and draw what you touched.

5. Make marks to show the shapes and **textures** that you felt.

6. Compare your drawing with the secret object!

Glossary

creative making something using your own ideas and how you feel inside

gallery place where art is displayed for people to look at

portrait picture of somebody

self-portrait picture that you draw of yourself

surface something that an artist draws on, such as paper

texture how a surface looks and feels

tools things you use to make art, such as pencils and crayons

Find out more

Book

Action Art: Drawing, Isabel Thomas (Raintree, 2005)

Website

Find out about Van Gogh's drawings and try making marks on this website:
www.metmuseum.org/explore/van_gogh/menu.html

Index

artists 4, 6, 9, 11, 13, 14, 16, 18, 19, 20

cartoons 15

colour 11

galleries 6, 23

ink 9

lines 4, 9, 10, 11, 17

museums 6

portrait 16, 18, 19, 23

self-portrait 18, 19, 23

shape 10, 11, 17, 22

texture 10, 22, 23

tools 8, 23